Charles Lucas

Seasonable Advice to the Electors of Members of Parlement

at the Ensuing Election

Addressed to the free and independent electors of the kingdom of Ireland

Charles Lucas

Seasonable Advice to the Electors of Members of Parlement at the Ensuing Election
Addressed to the free and independent electors of the kingdom of Ireland

ISBN/EAN: 9783337174996

Printed in Europe, USA, Canada, Australia, Japan

Cover: Foto ©Suzi / pixelio.de

More available books at **www.hansebooks.com**

SEASONABLE ADVICE

TO THE

ELECTORS

OF

MEMBERS of PARLEMENT

At the enfuing GENERAL ELECTION.

ADDRESSED

To the Free and Independent Electors of
the Kingdom of IRELAND in general,
to thofe of the City of DUBLIN in particular.

By CHARLES LUCAS.

Stand faft in the Liberty *wherewith* CHRIST *hath made you*
Free, and be not again intangled in the Yoke of Bondage.
ST. PAUL.

LONDON:

Printed for T. DAVIES, in Ruffel-Street, Covent-
Garden; J. COOTE, in Pater-nofter-Row; and
T. BECKET, in the Strand.
MDCCLX.

CHARLES LUCAS

To the FREE and INDEPENDENT
ELECTORS of the KINGDOM of
Ireland in general, to thofe of
the City of *Dublin* in particular ;
FREEDOM, HEALTH and PEACE :

My moſt dear Countrymen, worthy Fellow-
Citizens, and loving Friends ;

THOUGH long fevered from you,
by hateful and lawlefs oppreſſion,
I never was, nor ever can be, in-
attentive to your concerns. Silence would
but ill-become me on this important, this
critical conjuncture, big with events, which
muſt moſt nearly affect you ; events which
muſt, fooner or later, be felt by all Europe ;
I may ſay, by all the extremes of the globe.
Patiently hear me relate them. Call forth
all your fortitude : the firſt will tent you to
the foul : the good old king, that tender
and indulgent father of his people, over-
loaden with cares for the happineſs and glory

B   of

of his fubjects, anxious to put a ftop to human bloodfhed, and to give contending nations an equal, juft, and permanent peace ; his great heart, with inceffant labor in the common caufe, as it were, worn out, at length gave the fad proof of the mortality of the greateft of men.

I fee my mourning friends paying the laft tribute of loyal tears to the facred remanes of their deceafed fovereign ; I feel their fenfe of gratitude for his long paternal care of his people ; their refpect to his fteady valor, unfhaken juftice, and unparalleled clemency, and gladly applaud their awful reverence of the manifold perfonal and private virtues, which conftitute the royal character, and muft render his memory dear to generations yet unborn.

But, my friends, when time and reflection mitigate your griefs, you will thank heaven for the time and manner, in which your great king was called to a more exalted ftation, to change an earthly, temporal, for a glorious, eternal crown. It pleafed the ruler of princes to fpare this, his chofen delegate, in health of body and vigor of mind, till the moft diftant, as well as the neareft tyrants of the earth felt the terror of the arms of Britain ; it pleafed gracious heaven to fpare his precious life, till contending factions at home were filenced, till great offenders

were

were exemplarily punifhed and abafed, and till men of the firft abilities and merit were appointed to the moft honorable and important trufts; and above all, heaven was moft merciful in fparing his life, till the royal heir arrived at full age, well inftructed, and in all refpects well qualified to take up the reins of government. Thefe great points atchieved, without knowing a fingle infirmity of age, without any failure of his faculties, without a moment's pain, his great foul fhook off it's mortal coil, and fled to the blifsful manfions prepared for immortal heroes and for patriot kings.

Thefe juft obfequies to the manes of our departed king being payed, let us not forrow like men without hope; let us turn our eyes from the gloomy to the cheerful fcenes, by aufpicious providence prepared for the fenfible and loyal, for the legitimate fons of Great Britain and Ireland.

Now, my good friends, let me congratulate you on the fecond great event. Let your exulting hearts blefs heaven for bringing on the day of our redemption; for, fuch this event muft prove, if you remane as fenfible and as worthy of the bleffings of liberty, as you appeared when lawlefs force banifhed me from among you.

But, before I expatiate on the other great events, let me here expoftulate a while, with

fuch

such as may incline to derogate from the glories of the late regne, by pointing out the numberless complaints of our country and our city, which, so far from redress, still appear aggravated and complicated. It is most true, that not only delays, but open denials of justice, have frequently been made in the courts of law, probably by command of the great ; imprisoning men out of caprice, and denying them the benefit of the writ of original right, the *Habeas Corpus*, at the discretion or arbitrary will of judges or their rulers ; open obstructions given the execution of laws, and decrees or orders contrary to all laws, inforced by one of the three, without the concurrence of the two other, estates of the realm, without which there can be no law ; condemning innocent and loyal subjects unheared, and dooming them to gaols or banishment, without any rule or authority, without any form of law; and remitting such from a superior to an inferior court for further punishment, after passing a condemnation worse than death, in the former; the obstruction of the complaints of loyal subjects oppressed, and even punishing them for complaining ; the open sale of employments, ecclesiastical, civil and military, as well as of honors ; and that to the most worthless and infamous purchasers; and the multiplying of places and pensions for strangers

gers abroad ; or, what is ſtill worſe, as the wages of perfidy and corruption for impious parricides at home ; theſe are abuſes peculiar to our times, though ſhocking to every ſenſible, honeſt man. It is alſo true, that the general conduct of the king's lieutenants, from him who avowedly robbed the treaſury, leaving in it as he jocoſely, though wickedly declared, but *one crooked ſixpence*, down to him who ſwept it clean and involved You in an extravagant national debt, has been odious to every thinking man ; yet ſo far have all been from any degree of puniſhment or complaint of their adminiſtration, that the worſt of them returned with high rewards, and ſtill higher adulation, from your parlements to the royal preſence, even while the addreſſes of the people were not permitted to come to the royal ear: It is no leſs true, that claims have been laid, in the name of the crown, to unfortunate redundancies in the treaſury ; and the commons, for reaſons beſt known to themſelves, ſometime granted and ratified the demand, at the expence of equity, law, and truth, and of the inverting or overturning the eſſential forms of parlementary procedings. At another time, the ruling faction in the commons have found it convenient and neceſſary for their private purpoſes, to reſume their abandoned right, regardleſs of the precedent

cedent in a preceding parlement, yet without being mafters of the arguments to support their rights or thofe of the ill-reprefented nation ; and when they have refufed to give up thefe as before, the minifters of the crown have prefumed to lay their facriligious paws upon the undetermined fund, have taken the whole money, the bone of contention, out of the treafury, and difpofed of it by the fole authority of the prerogative!
———When addreffes or complaints to the throne have been by accident carried againft the fenfe of the miniftry, a Lord Lieutenant has been found, who dared to difpute the authority of the reprefentative of the nation, and obftruct the neceffary, free and frequent intercourfe that our government requires to fubfift between the king and parlement. Yet what punifhment was inflicted for fo daring an offence ? What motion was made againft the offender ?—None ; not even a motion was heared, upon the unparalleled occafion, but fuch as lukewarm fenators or hungry judges put, when cold or a keen appetite engages their attention, the cool motion of adjournment ! And inftead of any loud confequent complaint, the fhocking offence has been known afterwards privately, effectually, compromifed by the acting junto, without permitting a note upon the moft extraordinary proceding to be entered in the journals of the houfe !

houfe ! Thefe, with the overturning the conftitution of the capital city, though of matchlefs, unfhaken fidelity and loyalty, are but a
fmall part, the heads of the accumulated complaints of poor Ireland ! Thefe, could they
be occafioned by any king, muft undoubtedly have made him the object of the utmoft
contempt and indignation, inftead of the love
and reverence of a free people.

But, a little cool reflection muft ferve to
convince you, that the king, fo far from
authorifing or even countenancing fuch enormous oppreffions and grievances as thefe,
was artfully kept an utter ftranger to them
all, and was even made happy, with repet-
ed affurances of the florifhing ftate of his
loyal kingdom of Ireland. Thus, you find
all the addreffes of each houfe of parlement,
during this late regne, exulting in the great
happinefs and moft profperous ftate of the
kingdom. You find the royal clemency
greatly admired and applauded for fending
you the worft creature of the Britifh miniftry, much fuch a wretch as God gave in his
wrath, by way of a king, to curfe the moft
flavifh and corrupt people ; or fuch a log as
angry Jupiter fent to rule the frogs. And, at
the clofe of a feffion, You have never failed of
finding the moft fulfom, the moft extravagant adulation lavifhed upon the wifdom,
virtues and patriot adminiftration of one,
who

who acted more like an Oriental Nabob, or a Turkifh Captain Bafha, than the reprefentative of the limited Sovereign of a free people. If your vice-kings dare to obftruct or prevent the prefenting fuch parlementary addreffes as do not fuit their purpofes, to the throne ; how is it to be imagined, that the private complaints of the multitude, or the inflaved and beggarly condition of the whole country, can ever come to the ears of majefty ? You muft then be affured, that none of thofe impofitions and abufes, however enormous, however grievous and deftructive, could poffibly have been known, much lefs authorifed or countenanced by the king. There could be no regular accefs to his ear, in a national caufe, but from the parlement, your reprefentative, through the lieutenant, his majefty's reprefentative. If then, neither the king or you can be found to have had a reprefentative, how could your cafe be made known ? When you confider thefe maturely, you will join with me in pitying him, who with the unthinking or difaffected, is likely to bear the whole blame ; and you will of courfe, in common juftice, with me, turn your eyes and refentment on thofe, who appear to be the real authors of all your miferies. You will ufe your utmoft means to bring the perpetrators of thefe foul and deftructive deeds to condign punifh-

ment

ment and infamy, and fo redrefs your manifold and intolerable grievances; refcue the fame of your departed Sovereign from the glanced obloquy, and redeem the honor, and reftore the liberty and rights of a long oppreffed and plundered, loyal people. Thefe good things, you may now well and eafily atchieve; for, if it be not your own fault, the day of your deliverance is at hand.

. But, before I quit this fubject, I would have you all rightly conceive my fentiments on thefe matters, by which I hope we fhall be found to agree. I have been pretty explicit upon the fubject, in the dedication * of a tract of mine to the Prince, who now does honor to the throne; and there you may find an epitome of my political creed; as well as the following words, which you will permit me here to repete.——*I fhould think myfelf unworthy of enjoying thefe unparalleled benefits, could any means be able to efface the grateful fenfe of them, imprinted on my heart. —The jufteft of our politicians judge, that* Protection *and* Allegiance *are obligations mutual and reciprocal; between the* Governor *and the* Governed; *and that when the* one *is withdrawn, the* other *ceafes to be a debt.*—— *Yet pardon* mine *ambition to let your* Royal Highnefs *fee my fentiments of loyalty and gra-*

* Essay on Waters.

C   *titude*

*titude upon this occafion: Though I am, I
hope, the only fubject living, that can of a
truth complain of having been denied the* Protection, *that even criminals enjoy under our
laws, having notorioufly fuffered* the oppref-
for's wrongs, the law's delay, and the info-
lence of office, *to fay no more, and that without any tafte, or even profpect of redrefs; not-
withftanding, I can call upon my bittereft enemies to atteft, that it has not been in the
power of perfecution and adverfity to pervert
my fenfes, fo far as to make me impute the* un-
authorifed outrages *of* fubftitutes *to the* Principal, *or make me one moment difregard or
forget the* Deliverers *of my country, the* Re-
ftorers *and* Prefervers *of our moft* valuable,
our political health.——In this light, has the
ftate of the adminiftration ftruck me. And
though my conduct has made every fecret
and avowed enemy of the government mine,
without finding a fingle advocate among its
friends in power; yet I do, and muft per-
fevere in the fame fentiments, from a per-
fuafion of the juftice and equity of the proceding, not from either hopes or fears, having nothing to afk, nor any thing to fear,
while I can infure myfelf the calm funfhine
of a felf-approving confcience: a tribunal
which no power can fhake.

Thefe points being premifed and ftated,
let us now, my friends, change our doleful

dirges

dirges into the moſt heart-gladdening lays.
Take your long-unſtrung *harp from off the
weeping willows upon the banks of the waters
of* Babylon. Tune her to the moſt exquiſite
harmony, and let all free and loyal ſouls, oppreſſed, rejoice! for, the day of your deliverance is at hand. Bleſs God! and embrace it.
  Heaven be praiſed! We have lived to ſee
a prince aſcend the thrones of theſe realms,
adorned with every perſonal, with every
mental endowment, with wiſdom beyond
his years, and every virtue that can beſpeak
affection and reſpect, give luſtre to his
crowns, glory to his regne, or freedom and
happineſs to his people! A king, born and
bred a BRITON! who, though deſcended
of the good old ſtock, whoſe blood is de-
rived, through the pureſt channels, from
the moſt antient and illuſtrious race of So-
vereigns in Europe ; in the moment that he
aſcends the throne, deigns to claim our *regard*,
more by the endearing relation of *countrymen*, than to challenge our due *allegiance* as
ſubjects! Who calls *this, his native country!*
And while he is, with boundleſs, univerſal
joy, proclamed and confeſſed Sovereign,
vouchſafes to inroll himſeif a *Native*, a SON
of *Britain*, yea, to glory in the name of
BRITON! O! happy Iſle! at once the
mother and ſubject of a GREAT, a PA-
TRIOT KING!—This is he, whom I elſe-
where

where * pronounced, *born to disarm and to dissolve contending factions, to recover the lossed sheep of our fold; to call the prodigal children home, and to unite them in one family, infolded within the arms of a tender and indulgent parent, whom distant ages shall hail,* FA-THER OF HIS COUNTRY.——I have the royal word, solemnly given, to prove me a prophet, in this instance. They who know his Majesty's private and his princely virtues, want not this assurance of his great and good intentions towards his people. Such as have not that happiness must trust to his royal declaration, and his most gracious speech in parlement, from which all comforts, all hopes are to be drawn. For the information and satisfaction of my fellow-subjects of Ireland in general, for those of my worthy fellow-citizens in particular, I shall beg leave to transcribe the former royal words.

His MAJESTY's DECLARATION in Council, dated Oct. 25, 1760.

" The loss that I and the nation have sustained by the death of the king my grandfather, would have been severely felt at any time; but coming at so critical a juncture, and so unexpected, it is by many circumstances augmented, and the weight now fal-

* Same Dedication.

ling

...ng on me much increafed. I feel my own infufficiency to fupport it as I wifh. But animated with the tendereft concern for this my native country, and depending upon the advice, experience and abilities of your lord-fhips, upon the fupport and affiftance of every honeft man, I enter with cheerfulnefs into this arduous fituation, and fhall make it the bufinefs of my life to promote the glory and happinefs of thefe kingdoms, to preferve and ftrengthen the national conftitu-tion, both in church and ftate. And as I mount the throne in the midft of an expen-five, but juft and neceffary war, I fhall en-deavour to profecute it in the manner moft likely to bring on an honorable and lafting peace, in concert with my allies."

Was ever royal declaration fo dutiful! fo gracious! fo modeft! fo condefcending! fo pathetic! fo patriot! fo comforting! The glad fubjects now fee their *countryman*, their *king*, for the firft time fuch a bleffing has been enjoyed, in the memory of any, now living, in Britain. After paying the due re-gards to his deceafed grandfather and prede-ceffor, he declares his being *animated with the tendereft affection for* this his native coun-try. Then, *relies upon the advice, experi-ence, and abilities of his* COUNCIL, and calls *for the fupport and affiftance of every* HONEST MAN,

MAN, to enable him to difcharge his peculiar care, to complete the *great bufinefs of
his life, the promoting the glory and happinefs
of thefe kingdoms*, by preferving and ftrengthening the political conftitution.

Here, my drooping countrymen and
friends, here are fure grounds of comfort
and of hope, for all the fubjects, for you
efpecially, who want them moft ! here is
the GOLDEN BULL, that fecures you, Freedom and general happinefs, and your Sovereign, a glorious regne !—Your religion, your
liberties, all your concerns, now fall under
the royal attention and care! let this royal
declaration be engraved on the tables of your
hearts. Infcribe the facred words in letters
of gold under the pretious pourtrait or print
of your gracious fovereign, and teach your
lifping babes to read by it. And, for further affurance of the moral, religious, pious
intentions of his Majefty, fubjoin his royal
proclamation againft immorality, irreligion
and profanenefs, and add his moft gracious
fpeech from the throne. Are not thefe fuch
famples of an aufpicious, patriot, pious regne,
as roufe, revive, and call into action, every
moral, every political virtue in every breaft
among us ? You now can never fear finding
a known immoral or profane man, about
the facred perfon of your prince. And
when the evil counfillor is kept at diftance,
as well as *removed, from the* king, *his throne.*
                                          fhall

fhall affuredly *be eftablifhed*, as his regne has begun, *in righteoufnefs*. Every *honeft man* is now called upon to give *his fupport and affiftance* to facilitate the happy difcharge of the regal office. And what *honeft man*, with the fmalleft portion of fenfe, can deny his utmoft aid in carrying on the glorious work, in fharing in, and difpenfing to others, the ineftimable bleffings of A WISE AND VIRTUOUS ADMINISTRATION OF GOVERNMENT?— Whofe heart retains a fpark of generous liberty, and does not exult and bound within his breaft, at this godlike call? who does not pant with eager zeal to anfwer the godlike intentions of the king, in reftoring and confirming the civil and religious liberties of his people !

I hope we are all preparing, in our refpective vocations and ftations, to anfwer, to perform our parts, with becoming integrity, zeal and fortitude. Armed and furnifhed with thefe, my friends, we have all a right, it is our bounden duty, to advance, in our refpective fpheres. It were defertion, cowardice, perfidy, and treafon, to decline the charge.—It is true, my friends and brethren, we are not all born or bred, counfellors of ftate, politicians, heroes or foldiers. But there are, thank God! among us, many fenfible, honeft, loyal and brave men, of different vocations, in various ftations. And there is hardly any fo

mean,

mean, fo low, that has a moderate fhare of fenfe and honefty, who may not, in his fphere, in fome meafure, conduce to the forwarding and facilitating the great and arduous work of government, and fo anfwer the glorious invitation of his Sovereign, which is addreffed to EVERY HONEST MAN.

You, my moft dear and worthy countrymen and friends, who have long labored under the heavy weight of lawlefs oppreffion, without redrefs or comfort ; you, who are fo far removed from the reviving prefence of your Sovereign ; you are in a moft efpecial manner called on, upon this great occafion. Your gracious king addreffes you. Be not like the deaf adder, whofe dull *ears are fhut againft the voice of the* charmer, *charm* he *never fo wifely.* Or like thofe, who have long *fet in darknefs, and in the fhadow of death* ; yet *choofe darknefs rather than light, confcious of their deeds being evil.* Honefty is the cardinal qualification required, the virtue relied upon. Indeed it implies every other : for, an honeft man, in the extenfive acceptation of honefty, muft have all the focial virtues. He, knowing his duty, and his relation to all parts of the community, muft difcharge all the offices of life properly and juftly. His firft duty is to his country and to his king, which with us, hold infeparably one and the fame intereft. The honeft

honeſt man can never, conſiſtent with his character, deſert or decline the public ſervice, in
any inſtance, in any degree : his fortune and
his life are ever ready to be ſacrificed, when
the common good requires it. From the
ſame principles, the honeſt man acquits himſelf, uniformly and ſteadily, in all the offices
of ſociety. No wonder then, our wiſe and
gracious king calls on ſuch and ſuch onely,
knowing that ſuch muſt ever prove the onely
good members, the only ſure ſafeguard of
the ſtate. Hear then, my honeſt friends,
hear the charming voice of your king. He
calls forth all your manly virtues into action ;
bids, rather invites you, to exert them in the
common cauſe, in your own ſervice, for
ſelf-preſervation : for, a king capable of
making this declaration from his heart, can
have no view, no intereſt different from,
much leſs oppoſite to, that of his honeſt
ſubjects. He can enjoy no political happineſs, in which you have not the greateſt
ſhare. He knows, he is heaven's vice-
gerent, appointed not for his own ſole emo-
lument, but for the common good of all his
people. He can deſire no better a foundation for his thrones, than the pure affections
of ſenſible and honeſt, which muſt ever
prove loyal ſubjects, and founds the hopes
of a proſperous and glorious regne, upon
the freedom and happineſs, upon the glory

D   of

of the people committed to his royal care. Were ever subjects known so great, so happy? was integrity or probity ever known to have secured so ample a temporal reward, as when freedom, happiness and glory, assuredly attend her train?

Your sister Britain, who *actually* enjoys the blessing of a regne, which can onely be virtually extended to you, has manifold causes to exult in such a Prince's accession to the thrones. Yet, I must say, though it may seem a paradox at first, that Ireland has infinitely more: In Britain, it is to be presumed, that all parts of the government, in the late preceding regne, have been fairly and regularly administred. Here, are no complainings, no murmurings in the streets. Not onely bodies politic, but the meanest individuals are supposed to have equally and uniformly felt the salutary effects of a free dispensation of laws and justice with mercy, universally; while the sources of laws and mercy have been kept clear and unpolluted, in parlements, legally, freely, frequently convoked, impowered to act for a stated time onely, and actuated by the spirit and principles of the national constitution. These are blessings which have flowed from living, in some measure, within the reach of the royal eye. Blessings to which, you have been strangers.

You

You then, on whom the funfhine of majefty has not for centuries fallen, unlefs by
dull reflexion from fome fubftitute; You,
whofe true ftate and condition has never
been fully made known to your Sovereign ;
You, whofe laws are fpurned at, executed
or trampled under foot, as fuits the expedi-
ency of perfidious rulers and minifters; You,
whofe cities are difmantled or overturned,
whofe boroughs are depopulated, whofe
country is laid wafte, and whofe countrymen are daily fet a-begging, at the nod
of lawlefs power; You, whofe judges are
creatures, whofe places are dependent on
the breath of fome creating minifter;
you, whofe creatures and fervants have
long looked upon themfelves as your mafters ; whofe parlement has fet up for nothing lefs than perpetuity and omnipotence,
without any authority or countenance of
law or common fenfe ; while the different
eftates, inftead of acting in conjunction, as
one body, for the joint good of the whole,
have often affumed feparate powers, judica-
tive, legiflative, and executive, without
known bounds or reafon ; You, who have
feen fuch a long-lived, ftupendous monfter
often drain the vitals of the body politic, to
fupport fome lieutenant of the crown, or
creature of the miniftry here in that character, and his or their hungry minions and

fatelites,

fatelites, in luxury and extravagance, and in return, making many falfe reprefentations of the ftate of the nation, and permitting no juft remonftrance to be laid before the throne ; You, on whom the dregs of all evil governments have fallen, without having been once able to make your hateful and intolerable grievances known to your king ; You muft revive at feeing the deftructive *Hydra* flain by the YOUNG HERCULES : Your wounds and bruifes may now be dreffed and bound up, your inveterate putrifying fores may now be cleanfed, all healed, and new fpirits and vigor infufed into the whole diftempered, emaciated and almoft exhaufted body politic, and all its feeble and almoft paralytic members, by only attending in your refpective fpheres, to the divine calls of OUR COMMON POLITICAL FATHER, the true phyfician of the ftate, who offers an univerfal remedy for all your foul and complicate difeafes, if you have but political life and ftrength to bear its operation. He ftretches out the health-difpenfing hand, and offers you the vivifying fpirit of the Britannic conftitution. It is but drinking of it, as your forefathers did, and becoming HONEST, HEALTHFUL, VIGOROUS and FREE. You will pardon an unavoidable piece of pedantry.—And what return does your great benefactor expect at your hands, for this his invaluable

valuable gift? Your *support and affistance* under the weighty and arduous tafk of government, on which he depends to enable him
to complete the great *bufinefs of his life, to
promote the* HAPPINESS *and* GLORY *of his
people, to preferve and ftrengthen the* civil conftitutions of his kingdoms. O highly honorable and moft noble call ! O ! glorious tafk !
Heaven long preferve his invaluable life ! as
the fpirit of the conftitution ! the pride of
the people ! A reproach and fcourge to domeftic and foreign tyrants !

And now, you long-oppreffed fons of liberty, now refume and exert the fpirit of
your anceftors. The day of your probation or
deliverance is near at hand. Difpel the mifts
of ignorance and delufion ; caft off the hood-
winks that have been thrown before your
eyes, and gradually inure your organs, too
long weakened by impofed darknefs, inure
them timely to the light, leaft the fudden
darting of its unaccuftomed rays may fhock
the infeebled fenfes. The day is now near
at hand, when, my deareft countrymen and
friends are to ftand the great, the critical
teft. Your inviting King, and all the world
will foon fee, whether you dare be honeft,
happy, and free, or be grown perverfely or
habitually corrupt, and prefer wretchednefs,
flavery and contempt, to the fweets of virtue, to happinefs, to glorious liberty. It
will

will foon appear, whether the atrocious outrages committed on the whole body politic,
in which the facred political perfon of the
Sovereign fuffered, as well as fome innocent
and worthy individual members, in former
regnes, by lawlefs governors, corrupt counfellors, ignorant and fervile judges, ufurping
magiftrates, and packed perpetual parlements, be by you fenfibly felt, fpiritedly, loyally, honeftly, refented, now that the bonds
of your inflavers and their tyrannic powers
are to be fpeedily diffolved. The time is almoft come, when you are either to mani-
feft your fenfe, integrity and fpirit, and anfwer the calls of your Sovereign, by remon-
ftrating againft the prefent or paft and obviating future enormous impofitions and abufes, derogatory to the power, honor and
dignity of the crown, as well as infamoufly
injurious to your whole country; or whether
you purpofe to lye down, like dogs, con-
tented in hunger and eafe, with licking your
old wounds and fores, and playing in your
lothfome kennels, with chains by time and
confinement grown familiar and habitual.
But this is by no means to be fufpected.

If this were in any degree poffible, I fhould
fpurn you like dead dogs from my heart, from
my fight for ever. You could in no fort be intituled to any portion of any good man's care,
much lefs could you come within the letter

of

of our patriot king's gracious declaration.
His majefty wifely addreffes himfelf to the
nobleft work of God, the *Honeft man.* I
humbly follow the royal example. I know
multitudes of you, that dare be honeft, and
pant to be free. And I doubt not the majority of you will be univerfally found fuch
in the day of your probation. It is from this
affurance, and the calls of my king, that I
am roufed from the political lethargy, which
feized me at feeing no profpect of redrefs
of our national grievances. The profpect
now happily opening to our eyes, will, I
hope, cure you as well as me. Remember
then, my worthy friends, what I have fo
long laboured to inculcate, that every member of our community is by law, as well as
by nature, free. The fubjects of our crown
enjoy freedom, by the onely indubitable, in-
defeafable, hereditary right, acknowledged
among us. No man has a right by law to
diveft himfelf of the liberty inherent to him
as a member of the ftate. Liberty is the
political life of, every fubject. None can
give it up, without perfidy, treachery and
perjury, but in fuch portion and manner as
he forfeits it by the laws. So facred is the
liberty of every individual, that there exifts
no power, that can wreft it from the meaneft of the fubjects. No man can be deprived, by force, of his liberty more than of his
life,

life, without wounding the body politic of which he is a member. Therefore no man of fenfe, honefty, fpirit or loyalty, can confiftently fuffer his freedom or rights to be invaded in a fingle point, by any power whatever. Our king is injured when any of his fubjects are abufed. His power is only bounded in doing evil : He can do no wrong. Whereas, in doing good, his power knows no bounds. Among the regal attributes that give him the juft pre-eminence of all other potentates upon the earth, are thefe ; that while vaunting monarchs rule herds of flaves, fhackled by tyrannic force ; our fovereign governs a wife and free people by laws of their own framing, which are at once the meafure and the bond of allegiance and protection, the beft ftrength and fecurity of the prerogatives of the crown, and of the rights and liberties of the fubject. You, whofe beft and indefeafible birthright is liberty, can not be *flaves* and *honeft men.* Religion admits as well of fuicide, as law of felf-inflaving. Moreover, our king's honor and dignity can fuffer nothing more, than in ruling flaves. Our prefent gracious king *calls for* and *relies upon the fupport and affiftance of honeft men,* which *flaves* can never give. Thefe confiderations will undoubtedly roufe, my worthy fellow-fubjects, and fellow-citizens from fupinenefs and indolence, and make
them

them ufe every honeft, every lawful means, to recover their invaluable liberty, in what-foever inftance it fhall be found incroached upon ; it will engage him tò hand the na-tional conftitution *preferved and ftrengthened,* down, as it is his indifpenfible duty, to lateft pofterity.

I fee the effects thefe few inconnected ar-guments have upon you ; I feel the impref-fion, our King's godlike call, and the affur-ance of his great and patriot intentions have had upon you, my worthy countrymen, fel-low-citizens and friends. I gladly perceive the generous ardor, that warms each loyal breaft, and makes his depreffed heart pant for the inlivening fources of liberty. I ob-ferve you fpurn at the fhameful yoke, which has fo long galled your honeft necks. And it is evident, to your immortal honor, that you wifh for nothing more than the means of breaking the inflavers *bonds, and cafting off their cords from you.* And now, each free foul vies with the other, contending who fhall be foremoft in diftinguifhing his zeal in the caufe of his country, which is now his Sovereign's caufe ; the generous conteft is onely, who fhall give the patriot king the *firft* and *greateft fupport and affift-ance,* who fhall moft effectually coincide with the royal views, in reforming a lapfed or backfliding government, in reftoring, in

E   *pre-*

preferving and *ftrengthening the national conftitution, both in church and ftate.* You fee
the glorious opportunity, and you wait im-
patiently to fnatch up the means. Thefe
alfo are now happily prefented to your hands.
Think how juft, how great muft be your
condemnation, fhould any confideration de-
ter you from laying hold on the offered occafion of regaining the freedom and rights
of your kingdom, of your cities and boroughs; and fhould you, by any means, be
brought to fail, in this the great day of your
deliverance, in anfwering the glorious calls
of your king and country. If you fail now,
you may poffibly bid farewel for ever to all
the profered bleffings.

You muft all, my friends, be fenfible,
that all the grievances under which you have
long groaned, have arifen from the ignorance, fupinenefs, cowardice, or corruption
of too long-lived parlements: Thefe have
ever run in with, and given fanction to, the
worft meafures of the worft rulers that have
at any time been fent to fcourge and to plunder the kingdom. It muft ever have been
the intereft and care of fuch, to cut off all
intercourfe between the king and his oppreffed people ; and confequently, as the parlement fixed its own duration upon the ftand-
ard of the king's life, the length of the king's
life, which the other kingdom looked for as

a

a blefling, to you muft have proved the moft dreadful evil; as it always prolonged the duration, extended the powers, and ferved to encourage the corruption of a democracy, the worft of all tyrannies when corrupt, beyond all tolerable bounds. Thank providence! we never had fo good a profpect of a long, indeed of a glorious regne, as now. Shall Ireland be the onely part of the dominions of our crowns, that fhall not have caufe to pray for a long and profperous regne to the king? If you have but the fenfe and virtue to choofe juft reprefentatives, wife and honeft counfilors to the crown, and faithful guardians to your country, you will be alike interefted with the reft of the fubjects, in the king's long life. But, at this diftance, what can all his royal virtues, all his public fpirit and patriot intentions avail, if you be not honeft enough to appoint worthy reprefentatives?—If for want of thefe, you have fuffered fo long and fo much, in the laft long-lived parlement, though under a moft juft and gracious king; you can blame none but yourfelves, if the like evils fhould happen under this regne. And, you muft reafonably expect, that Britain will have the prudence, for felf-prefervation, to ftretch out her arms, to ward off the infecting peftilence; or you may yourfelves be neceffitated to beg for that moft violent and defperate remedy,

medy,

medy, which you now so justly dread, an Union. Fools are not to be trusted with fire-brands among combustibles. And infants and lunatics are not to be trusted with the care and management of their own estates, when they may waste and abuse them to the prejudice of their posterity, as well as to that of their neighbours. A word to the wise. Be wise, my friends, before it be too late; be honest, happy and free!

The great and long-wished for occasion of our redemption being so near at hand, every individual, should prepare and set every engine to work, that may possibly contribute to the desired end. You must know that it can never be possible for every individual to gain personal access to the king. But, that none individual should possibly suffer by this, our wise ancestors provided, that each of the small divisions of the societies which compose our commonwealth, should be inabled to send chosen delegates, representatives, to serve for them in the assembly of the states of the nation. These, we have, in the excellencies of all the best known forms of human governments, monarchy, without tyranny, aristocracy, without oligarchy, and democracy, without anarchy, in our king, lords and commons, which constitute our great and glorious commonwealth; a constitution, in which the respective powers, prerogatives, and privileges

vileges of the head and members are afcer-
tained and blended, in fuch juft, fuch equal,
fuch attemperating proportions, as balance,
ftrengthen and fecure the whole, and leave
none of the conftituent parts, not even the
inferior limbs of our body politic, room to
repine at his lot ; fince the meaneft is as fecure, as free, in his low, as the greateft, in
his exalted, fphere ; and the laft, as well as
the firft, gives his confent, in his proper perfon, or by his reprefentative, to the fyftem
of laws, by which he is, at once, governed
and protected *.

Thus then, my friends and brethren,
thus you have all a right to gain accefs to
the throne, and *to council*, *to fupport*, and *to
affift* your king. See the honor, fee the
truft, fee the importance of the moft ob-
fcure or inferior ftations ! See what glory
and happinefs muft attend the wife and juft
difcharge of the duties of your fpheres ! See
what infamy, what wretchednefs and reproach attend the ignorance, neglect or abufe
of your great duty, and the weighty truft re-
pofed in you, which is not onely for the prefent, but for future ages ! Think of thefe
things, and fee if you can intruft a fool or a

---

* See my dedications of the great charter of Dublin
to the King, and of mine Effay on Waters, to the
Prince ; and my *Political Conftitutions of* Great Britain
and Ireland.

knave

knave with matters of the greateſt importance, without riſquing every loſs, and falling
under the imputations yourſelves of being no
wiſer or honeſter than the repreſentative you
have appointed by a public choice. Cun-
ning knaves may ſend a thief to catch a thief.
But he muſt be a fool indeed, that ſends a
fool of his errand. This, I hope, can never be the caſe in Ireland.

With an exulting heart, I moſt ſincerely
congratulate you, my dear countrymen and
fellow-citizens, on the approaching diſſolu-
tion of a parlement, which can hardly be
ſayed to have anſwered any of the ends of its
inſtitution, much leſs to have *ſupported and
aſſiſted* their ſovereign in his patriot intentions of *promoting the glory and happineſs* of
his people. That this has not been done, you
all have reaſon to lament, as well as I, but
moſt eſpecially you, my honored and beloved fellow citizens, who have been ſtripped
of your eſtates and franchiſes, and denied the
exerciſe of the common funćtions of free
men, particularly in the important points of
electing your magiſtrates, as well as members to repreſent you in the common council both of the city and nation. Witneſs the
unheared of obſtructions given to you in the
laſt general election for your city, the preventing your electing the citizen you pitched
upon, the turning out one whom you had
moſt

moft fairly, regularly and indifputably elected, and the impofing one upon you, whom
you neither did, nor upon your principles,
poffibly could at any time, elect. What
king could obviate or remedy this fhocking
abufe? Who then is to be fuppofed juftly to
bear the blame? The electors or the elected,
or both.

I have, in the *political conftitutions of*
Great Britain and Ireland *afferted and vindi-
cated*, in the *apology* for the *civil rights* and
liberties of the commons and citizens, in the
complaints of *Dublin*, delivered to, and
fuppreffed by, one of the chief governors,
and in my *Dedication* of the tranfcript and
tranflation of your Great Charter to the late
king, fairly and fuccinctly layed down the
legal conftitutions of thefe realms, together
with that of your city; and have layed down
and demonftrated, beyond all room for con-
tradiction, the fatal incroachments and in-
fringements made in the national conftitution of Ireland, as well as in that of her capital, down to the time, in which I was forced into exile. So far from any attempt to
deny the charges, the aggreffors themfelves
have upon many occafions been forced to confefs them. How far thefe fhocking breaches
have been inlarged, and with what aggrava-
tion fince my banifhment, muft be obvious
to every thinking man. Has there been any
over-

overture, any attempt to redrefs the general grievances? No; not one, that I can learn, except a pitiful palliative for fome abominable oppreffions in the city, agreed upon to filence the clamor of the abufed citizens, and to fecure a fhare of popular favor to thofe who got the paltry bill paffed, throwing out one that was more rationally framed, and that upon a fhameful compromife. It is then, evident to demonftration, that all the evils, of which the nation or the city complain, were brought on and confirmed by a combination of avaricious, wicked rulers with fpurious reprefentatives, immerged in ignorance, fupinenefs or corruption; appointed by ignorant, feduced, corrupted or inflaved conftituents, or cruelly impofed upon the honeft and free electors, by falfe commons, impudently arrogating to themfelves the pernicious power of appointing members, or licencing elections, for all parts of the kingdom, as the feats happened to become vacant.——— Under thefe fad circumftances, what part of the kingdom could fay, it was fairly or legally reprefented in parlement? Poor Dublin, in particular, what reprefentatives have you had? O! name them not!———Where then could the moft gracious king look for all that ours now afks, *the fupport and affiftance of honeft men, in promoting the* glory *and* happinefs *of thefe* confederate *kingdoms?*

How

How could he obviate, how redrefs your grievances?——How was it poffible to pre-ferve and ftrengthen the civil conftitution? You could not all have given him your perfonal affiftance; you could have given your council and your aids by your dele-gates alone. How far then were our mem-bers or thofe impofed upon us for fuch, qua-lified, in any fenfe, to anfwer the king's moft gracious demands and patriot views? or to reprefent a fenfible, honeft, loyal and free people? When did thefe reprefentatives lay a true ftate of the nation before the throne? When complain of the evil conduct of jud-ges and governors? Or were the worft of thefe, in our days, diftinguifhed by the com-mons, but by excefs of adulation? It could not be otherwife. A confederacy is foon formed by men of correfponding fentiments and views. Few have been follicitous for the regency of Ireland, but for felfifh views. Few have folicited or obtained feats in the Irifh parlement, upon better principles or with lefs interefted views. To fulfil the in-tentions of fuch governors and fuch com-mons, a co-operation was neceffary, and this was never known to fail, while each had a fatisfactory fhare of the booty of the plun-dered. The pliant commons were tenderly and refpectfully fpeeched by the ravenous governor, and while thofe were gratified

with

with places, pluralities and penfions, or with honors dearly, hardly bought, at the expence of fenfe and virtue, as well as of cafh; the governor was always reprefented to the king with the wifdom of Solomon and the integrity of Cato, and the kingdom florifhing, great, happy and free. And thus thefe confederate potentates reciprocally tickled and flattered each other, while the people were ever undone by the confederacy. What king, that was not more than a mortal, could poffibly prevent, know or forefee thefe evils? Or remedy the unknown grievances, when moft heavily inflicted on the people?

If then all your unfpeakable, complicated grievances, your wounds and bruifes, your ftripes and bonds, your oppreffion, beggary and difgrace, be, as muft be confeffed, thus apparently inflicted by evil governors, corrupt counfilors, and fpurious perrennial parlements; the king can never fee, or be any ways made fully acquainted with the calamitous circumftances of his people, and confequently, cannot interpofe to fave you from utter deftruction. And thus, you at once fee, that no King can be blamed for your paffed or future fufferings, till you fhall have recourfe to the onely poffible means of redreffing your wrongs and vindicating your honor, the appointing fit reprefentatives, which, to be legitimate, muft be wife and virtuous,

honeft

honeſt and free. Such and ſuch onely can fulfil the juſt purpoſes and expectations of the people, and the patriot intentions of his majeſty, by yielding that *ſupport and affiſtance*, which *honeſt men* alone give, and which is ſo eſſentially neceſſary to enable the ſovereign *to promote the* glory *and* happineſs *of his people.* Theſe good ends can only be accompliſhed by frequent and free elections of a juſt national repreſentative, which will ever keep up a conſtant and regular intercourſe with the crown, ever acquainting the ſovereign with the genuine ſenſe of the people, and whatever paſſes in the kingdom. And thus repreſented and governed, you would never be permitted to feel your diſtance from the throne.

Now, my worthy friends, let the ax be layed to the root of the tree, and let every rotten or ſtunted tree, or ſuch as is found incapable of bearing its due proportion of wholeſome fruit, be cut off and rejected. As the tree is known by its fruit, ſo with the conſtituents, by their repreſentatives. Such electors as are duly qualified to anſwer the patriot king's call, ſuch as are wiſe and virtuous, honeſt and free, muſt inevitably chooſe and delegate members, worthy of themſelves; true repreſentatives; men that bear the teſtimony of their legitimate miſſion about them; they muſt be *ſenſible, diſintereſted, honeſt* and *free*; ſuch as are capa-

F 2   ble

ble and determined to affert your rights and
vindicate your wrongs, againſt the higheſt
powers, as well in the ſenate, as the field ;
ſuch as have heads ſo clear, and hearts ſo
upright, ſo firm, that the king may ſee your
ſenſe, honeſty and loyalty in them, and with.
ſafety rely on you in them, for *ſupport and
aſſiſtance* in his great, patriot intentions of
promoting the happineſs and glory of his
people, by *preſerving and ſtrengthening* the
national conſtitution.

On the other hand, thoſe who have not
the ſenſe, integrity or fortitude neceſſary to
make the juſt and neceſſary choice, will ſuf-
fer ſenſeleſs dolts, or artful and deſigning
knaves to be impoſed upon them, as mock-
repreſentatives, or will be baſe enough to
ſell their birthrights for a meſs of potage,
to the firſt ſordid purchaſer that offers.
Theſe may clog, but never can promote the
meaſures of any wiſe and righteous government, but leſt of all, thoſe of a patriot adminiſtration, as ours happily is, at this day.
And thoſe, if any there be, who are weak
or wicked enough to attempt to mar the unparalleled freedom and happineſs which await
us in this auſpicious regne, by returning any
of the ſons of pride or iniquity to the great
council of the ſtate, deſerve puniſhment beyond any that our mild government can in-
flict upon the moſt atrocious offenders.   Let
bonds

bonds and infamy in a foregne ſtate, be their portions on earth! But why ſhould I mention ſuch deteſtable characters, as I hope will be no more heared of in our iſles? I gladly quit the painful view. And now,

Thank heaven! my friends, inſtead of any unſurmountable obſtacles, we have every incentive, to a wiſe and free election of well qualified repreſentatives, in this auſpicious regne. You are not now called to return members to an houſe of commons, as inſolent, as arbitrary in their procedings, whoſe tyrannic rulers preſume to dictate *a Congè d'elire*, peremptorily point out whom you ſhall, and whom you ſhall not chooſe, or haughtily impoſe ſuch members as they liſt upon you. Praiſed be Providence! it now is yours to form a new, a conſtitutional houſe of commons, a true and reſpectable repreſentative of the nation. Such muſt prove wiſe counſilors to the king, and faithful guardians of his free peoplè. Such alone can regain your loſſed rights. Such alone can reſtrain or puniſh evil ſubſtitutes of the king, ſhould any ſuch be hereafter appointed. Such alone can coincide with the patriot intentions of the king. On ſuch alone, he can ſafely rely for *ſupport and aſſiſtance* in his government. Such muſt ever keep up a conſtant, free and regular intercourſe with the Sovereign, without letting

you

you ever feel your real diftance from the throne. Such will ever give due encouragement and protection to arts, fciences, manufactures and commerce, and every laudable induftry. Such will difcountenance and fupprefs public, as well as private, luxury and prodigality. And, if by any unforefeen accident, an unworthy fubftitute fhould hereafter happen to be fent to hold the reins of government amongft you; fuch a reprefentative would be able to fhield you from the baneful effects of a corrupt adminiftration ; would fupply an effectual prefervative againft the peftilential infection of his evil morals in private, or his evil politics in public, life. Such a fubftitute fhould not be able to rob the treafury, or to involve the nation in debts. He fhould not be able to fhock public credit, or to fupprefs trade. And much lefs, fhould he dare to fcourge you with fcorpions, or to rule you with a rod of iron. Nor fhould he be able to mifreprefent you to the crown, or to intercept or prevent your complaints being layed before the throne. Upon the firft overture of fuch attempts, the juft reprefentative, ever fupported by their free and loyal conftituents, would readily ftop the moft rapid carreer of the moft powerful and iniquitous ruler. They would gag or muzzle, draw the teeth, or muffle the plundering paws of

fuch

fuch a beaft of prey, and for further punifhment, would remit him to his offended and
abufed principal, with the full proofs of his
crimes againft the Sovereign and his people ;
or, by their own authority, a brave reprefentative would bring fuch an audacious de-
linquent to his trial and juft condemnation
in the proper courts. It is to be hoped,
that you were never curfed with fuch rulers.
And I dare affirm, you will never fee fuch,
till you appear corrupt and inflaved enough
to deferve no better, by delegating your
powers and privileges in parlement to the
fons of pride, folly or corruption. Should
that ever be the cafe, the worft treatment
due to rebels and traitors, would be too
good for you. But, thank God ! thefe can
never be.

Now then, my worthy brethren and
friends, now, that all obftacles to the regaining, preferving, ftrengthening and per-
petuating your freedom and rights are removed ; now, that nothing is wanting but
the proper exertion of fenfible heads and
honeft hearts, to fulfil our good king's great
intentions of *promoting and cftablifhing the
freedom, the happinefs, the glory* of his fubjects, univerfally, and without diftinction ;
can any man with- hold the fupport and affiftance required, confiftent with the love and
duty he owes his country, himfelf or pofterity,

rity, with the regard due to the moſt gracious of ſovereigns, who, with the ſtretched-
out arms of a moſt tender and indulgent parent, relying on your integrity, invites you not
only to contribute your aid, but to a ſhare in
the government! to happineſs! to glory! to
liberty! ---- After this, who can ſhew himſelf
ſuch a ſtupid ſlave, or abandoned profligate,
as not to exert his utmoſt might in ſecuring
theſe invaluable bleſſings, by returning wiſe
and virtuous repreſentatives, on which the
very eſſence of our moſt excellent government depends? Let not ſuch a worthleſs
wretch live among honeſt free men!

I am perſuaded, that my worthy countrymen and fellow-citizens will duly priſe, and
not let ſlip, this invaluable opportunity of
diſcharging, with becoming zeal, freedom
and fortitude, the moſt important of all the
truſts repoſed in men. Who lives, that can
ſay, he may ever ſee ſuch another opportunity? Who can have a right to hope for
another, or can deſerve ſuch another gracious offer, that does not gladly accept of
theſe, and improve them to the utmoſt ad-
vantages, intended or wiſhed? If evil rulers
and counſilors ſhould again conſpire with
falſe, perpetual repreſentatives, and both
ſhould again interpoſe between you and
your Sovereign, and again cut off the neceſſary intercourſe between a free people and
the

the crown ; remember that the long life, the wifdom, and all the patriot virtues of your king, could avail you nothing ; another eclypfe, fuch as you have lately got clear of, may exclude you all light, fo long, fo effectually, as to make pofterity ignorant of their being intituled to the comforts of the left gleam, or even to a fingle ray.

It is high time, my countrymen and friends fhould emerge from the fhameful infignificant and wretched ftate, in which you have dragged on a lingering life for years paffed. It is time to hear the calls of virtue, of liberty, of your country. Thefe your gracious king loudly makes. Will you not hear him? Will you not fly to anfwer him?—I know you will. Let then, every virtuous man blefs his God, thank his king, and joyoufly accept the happinefs and glory profered to him, to his country, to pofterity. Let him prepare to furnifh the grand council of the realm with thofe faithful reprefentatives, on whofe fenfe and honor, both king and conftituent, may fafely rely. To this end, let him freely examine the characters of candidates in general. And more efpecially, let him bring the conduct of late reprefentatives to the ftricteft trial, by the exact balance of truth and reafon. Let him learn and judge what they have done, or caufed or fuffered to be done, for, or againft,

the

the true and infeperable intereft, honor and happinefs of their king and country, in the late, long parlement. Inquire how they came by their feats in parlement, and why they prefumed to hold them, againft the fpirit and the very effence of the civil con-ftitution, for a term of years unknown in, and contrary to, law. If there be any that have gained free and honorable elections, and have difcharged the delegated truft with proper zeal and integrity, and a true defe-rence to their conftituents, and no doubt, there are many; though they fhould be ignorant of the evil or unlawfulnefs of prolonging the parlement beyond juft and legal bounds, the electors fhould be un-animous in re-electing them. But, every elector fhould fet an indelible mark on thofe who are found to have purchafed feats, for private convenience, and efpecially thofe, who by falfe petitions and finifter in-fluence in the houfe, have got the lawful reprefentative rejected, and the fpurious im-pofed upon the abufed conftituents. Here is fuch an evil, fuch a complication of crimes, as fingly taken, are each of the deepeft dye that guilt can give. Whoever would truft fuch a man with the conduct of his part of the government, cannot be much wifer than he who would commit the care of his houfe and fortune to common thieves. Such men can never feek a feat in parlement with

any

any fort of honeft views. The ordinary motives of fuch men are eafily learned by their circumftances and conduct; they procure feats by the moft illicit meafures, and at great expence, to get fkreened, by the fhameful abufe of parlementary privilege, from juftice and law, to the ruin of honeft, induftrious creditors, or which is ftill worfe, to barter their venal voices to the difhonor of parlement and the deftruction of their reprefentatives ; while they infamoufly extort the wages of their iniquity from the plunder of their unhappy ward, the people. Such falfehood, fuch perfidy, fuch hardy proftitution has fometime been known to have exhaufted the public revenues and difgraced your ftate. You tremble and ftand aghaft at the bare recital ! —— No wonder; it fhocks the ear. Who has dared to oppofe thefe deftructive meafures ? Who dared to tell the important truth ? ——I dare not concele it. Look to it then, my friends ; fee that you exclude fuch perfidious flaves the fenate ; try for means to fever the corrupted limbs from the found body, as you hope to efcape the infection, and to live honeft and free. This is the time to exert yourfelves. You know your duty to your king and country, to yourfelves and pofterity. Take care you do not defert your pofts, in the day of trial. And be affured,

that

that he is no better than a perjured traitor, who on this critical emergency, with-holds or declines giving the fhare of *affiftance and fupport* he may afford to the redeeming and reforming the public adminiftration.

Let me earneftly warn you, my honeft friends, againft electing the domeftic officers or fervants of any chief governor, or any of the numerous train of ftrange or native vaffals, that live upon the garbage about a fecond-hand court. Think how many of thofe have, by fome bafe means or other, got feats in your parlement, within thefe thirty-three years, who attended onely at their mafter's will and command, and were never feen in the houfe, when his regne ended and his purpofes were ferved. Such can never be the legitimate reprefentatives of an honeft and free people. Nor was it ever intended they fhould. It is your faults if fuch ever find footing in your councils again.

You cannot, my worthy fellow-fubjects, confiftent with your characters and duties, choofe reprefentatives among the numberlefs placemen that difgrace and exhauft the ftate. Not one of thefe is eligible into a feat in parlement, whofe employment is not of importance to the public, and whofe conduct in this, as well as in the legiflative capacity, if called to it, has not been found fenfible,

fenfible, upright and independent. It is
your intereft and duty to look upon all
placemen in general, with a fufpicious, with
a jealous, diftruftful eye. And you fhould
ftrictly charge and require your reprefentatives to bring in a bill to afcertain the qualifications, and to limit the number of placemen in parlement. In Britain, a member's
accepting of a place, vacates his feat. This
gives the conftituents an opportunity of re-
electing or rejecting him, according to his
behaviour. Why may not Ireland have
fuch a bill ?

As for the whole impious band of penfioners, thofe drones who confume the fruits
of the labors of the induftrious, thofe pa-
rafites, who live by fucking out the vitals
of a confumptive ftate, truft not one of
them in parlement, and ufe all means to
have them ftruck off the fhameful and deftructive lift ; unlefs where you find them
fuperannuated, maimed or broken in the
faithful fervice of their country, or by having otherwife well and loyally deferved fuch
a reward at your hands. Where you find
them worthy of fuch gratifications, it would
be but unjuft to deprive them. But, the
very name of *penfioner* or *dependent* fhould
totally difqualify any man for being the
reprefentative of an honeft and free people.
If you find your ftate burthened with a
fwarm

swarm of thefe locufts, it is a fure proof of a diftempered commonwealth. Thefe will generally be found the children of corruption, who thrive and multiply like flies and maggots, when there is the greateft plenty of carrion. In general, you muft avoid choofing them your members, as you would fhun a peftilence, and ufe your utmoft influence to get all the undeferving, worthlefs penfioners cut off, for the honor and eafe of the king and the fubject.

Next to thefe, you will prudently caft your eyes upon the immenfe number of lucrative offices, many of which are as ufelefs as burthenfome to the fubject, granted by patent, not onely for the life of the incumbent, but fometimes for a generation or two longer. Such grants as thefe muft be prefumed to have been furreptitioufly obtained, when the commons were found void of fenfe and integrity, and fuffered many things difhonorable and injurious to the crown and fubject to be done, without having the virtue to give their faithful council to the king. If a king may grant one employment in reverfion, why not all ? If all be made over in reverfionary grants, what is left to the difpofal of the fucceffor ? May he not thus be deprived of the neceffary and juftly inherent power of appointing his own minifters, officers and fervants ? And can any of our

kings

kings deprive the fucceffor of the difpofal of the employments about his court, with greater reafon and juftice than he can alienate the royal patrimony? Could a true friend to the crown, or the fucceffor, advife or accept fuch an alienation? Muft not a wife and virtuous national reprefentative confider all reverfionary grants, efpecially in Ireland, in this light? And, if they find the crown or the kingdom burdened with fuch, upon duly weighing the charaĉters of the grantees, and the means ufed to obtain fuch reverfions, would it not be thought moft reafonable and equitable to refcind all clandeftine grants, and to reftore them to the 'injured fucceffor, by a general aĉt of refumption? What heir would think himfelf bound by a leafe or grant of an eftate, made by his father, while, by unalterable fettlements, he was made tenant for life?——But, be this as it may, beware of choofing reprefentatives among this clafs of men. You muft look upon their places in general as furreptitioufly obtained from the crown by fome artful defigning minifter, as a reward to fome of his fervile creatures. There is no general rule, without an exception. I hope, you will be able to prove this a general rule, by proving that fome grantees are exceptions. But you can not properly eleĉt thefe, more than any other placemen,

But,

But, be that as it may, if any be found among you, who, under a corrupt or tyrannical adminiſtration, obtained penſions, commiſſions or places, whether for life, or during the pleaſure of the miniſter, and thoſe as the wages of any known or ſecret, illicit ſervice ; the greateſt lenity you can ſhew ſuch ſhameleſs ſlaves, and the leſt proof you can give of your own public ſpirit and regard to juſtice and the calls of your ſovereign, is to prevent ſuch offenders being any where, ſo much as named candidates. The tainted breath of ſuch parricides is enough to taint the air you breath, or to bring a curſe upon a whole ſtate. Remember, it is an inſult to your ſovereign, as well as an indelible diſgrace, and may prove an irretrievable detriment, to yourſelves and to your country, to return any for your members, who are not *honeſt, independent* and *free.*

I have now, my worthy friends, briefly enumerated certain claſſes of men, by the principles of our polity, and by common ſenſe, abſolutely diſqualified for the offices of repreſentatives in parlement. Let me now caution you further in your choice.

Be cautious of every man, who is very ambitious to obtain a ſeat in parlement, eſpecially if he ſtoops to any degree of illicit or ſiniſter means to obtain it. The views of ſuch men muſt ever be ſuſpected. The ſeat of

a mema member can be no lucrative office to an honeſt man. And few, too few, will be found to ſeek the trouble from pure diſinte-reſted, from patriot views.

I hope, you are aware of the many little deſpicable artifices, practiſed by ſome ſhal-low knaves to impoſe upon you, that you may put them into offices, where they may expoſe themſelves. How many juſtices and jurors, how many chief and other magiſtrates of cities and boroughs have I ſeen, running into all the low extremes of follies and even petty oppreſſions, onely to gain the ill-found-ed fame of being active and diligent in the diſcharge of their offices? Thus the mayor, in whoſe time the largeſt loaf was ſold, either from the plenty of corn, or at the expence of the poor, innocent, oppreſſed baker; or he who ſeized moſt bread and butchers meat, though with the leſt appearance of juſtice or law; and he who ſtopped or pul-led down encroaching buildings, or moſt inſolently terrified his innocent neighbours, contrary to all rules and forms of law; ne-ver fails of demanding a triumph in any corporation, not even in Dublin. Almoſt every one of theſe annual Baſhas is a great legiſlator and a perſuaſive orator, in his own imagination; while he hardly underſtands, and cannot for his ſoul deliver, common ſenſe, in plane Engliſh! I have heared of a judicial officer ſtoop to the moſt miniſterial, mean, manual offices, and afterwards pub-liſh his hardy indecent deeds in print, to re-commend him to ſome degree of the favor of a populace, by belying and abuſing of which he was forced into one of their ſeats in parlement, and by thus publiſhing his ſhame, hoped to gain favor enough to keep his ill gotten place, by ſhewing he could be active, in ſpight to his paunch, though he could never arrive at any thing ſenſible or decent. Who hears this, that does not recollect the humorous fable of the aſs and the ſpaniel? I have heared of ſome juſtices, who never did right, for fear of doing wrong. While others reverſe the caſe, and are al-ways doing wrong, fearing they ſhould ne-ver happen to be able to do right. Who can chooſe ſuch, that is not capable of ſend-ing a fool of his errand?

Lawyers in general, the council and re-corders of cities in particular, think that, from their learning and abilities, they are well qualified, and by their public and pri-vate ſervices, well intituled to gain the voi-ces of ſenſible and honeſt freemen, upon an election. The preſent recorder of the city, from the great zeal of him and his family in eſtabliſhing and protecting the uſurpations of the aldermen, lately thought he had ſe-cured an intereſt ſufficient to pack him into parle-

parlement. He knew, it was one of the neceſſary ſteps towards a lawyer's promotion. And, to prove his titule and his qualifications, he publiſhed Letters, which ſhew his riſing parts, I dare ſay, in a very fair light. His great ſervices in prevaling upon one city member, by way of compromiſe, to give up a ſenſible bill brought in for the regulation of the city, and to accept in its place, a lax and inſignificant one of his drawing, he judges muſt ſecure an election to him and his maſter and pupil, the alderman. Perſuaded of this, he need but ſet forth his clame by way of an appendix to a new edition of his letters. But, wiſe and honeſt men are not to be taken by ſuch tranſparent baits as theſe. Are my countrymen and fellow-citizens perſuaded of the tranſcendent merit of the learned gentlemen of the long robe? or are you ſenſibly indebted to thoſe that are or have been in the houſe, for the virtuous diſcharge of the duties of ſtateſmen or ſenators? If the eminent judges of the late queen were living, they could anſwer this queſtion to your ſatisfaction. We can not ſay, there was *none honeſt, no not one* among them. One, indeed, and but one, was found. What the judges in earlier times were, you have ſeen ſet forth in the complaints of Dublin. But, if you ſtill remane in doubt about the great qualifications and ſteady patriot virtues of the

lawyers.

lawyers, turn your eyes up to the wife and worthy fages, that now do honor to the benches in your courts, or to the learned and refpectable gentlemen, in and out of the houfe, who with becoming humility, modefty, and equal integrity and patriotifm, humbly afpire at thefe honorable places. I remember a venerable lawyer, who from a zealous patriot, became a courtier, when the moft interefting queftion was depending in parlement, upon onely being told by a Lord Lieutenant, that a judge's robes would fuit this barrifter well, and that he was interefted in knowing how baron Pocklington was, who perhaps was bid to fham ficknefs for the purpofe. This ingenious, temporary patriot did not, it is true, receive the expected wages. Though you may think he got as much as he deferved, when derifion and contempt drove him from the bar, with the nick-name of baron, which will ftick to him to his grave.

Some, I hear there are, to whom parts feem to have been given as a curfe to themfelves and to their country, who lay clame to the applaufe and voices of a free people, for the diligent difcharge of a great employment. If this place be attended with an adequate reward, the public debt is furely payed to this great officer. But, the keeping of his employment may perhaps depend
upon

,pon his having a feat in parlement. Is it then incumbent on an honeft, free people to choofe him in order to fecure his place? Inquire how this great man got his feat and his place, and fee for what purpofes he purchafed the one, and on what confiderations he firft got a large penfion, which he afterwards got converted into a lucrative employment. If you fhould find fuch a fellow proftituting himfelf, by contriving and perpetrating every foul or wicked machination of the worft. of minifters, firft for private bribes, and at laft for a public profitable place ; if you fhould find his firft rife fpring from no lefs a crime than the affaffination of innocence, which could not be perpetrated, without giving a fatal wound to the body politic ; could you fuffer fuch an odious flave, off whom the provoked populace could once hardly keep their hands ; could you permit the impious, well-payed parricide to be once named at an election ? O ! no, it is impoffible ! Then as to his difcharge of his office, it will be found not much more meritorious. If it be true, that he is moft active and ftrict; yet every judicious man will find, what foregne merchants exclame at, that in ftraining at gnats, he fwallows camels. That he lays trade under fuch difficulties, reftraints and delays, as perhaps caufe fome increafe of the revenues, with

refpect

refpect to one fhip. But, if a fhip might make four trips, while thus fhe can make but three, would it not be better for the private trader and for the public? and would it not anfwer as well for the revenue to gain, for example, four times three-pence, as three times four-pence? then, if this be the cafe, what greater merit has this man, than diligence and activity, ill-applied in his place? can fuch a man be a fit object for your choice? no; it is impoffible. Let him remane in his employment, if you will; but he never can be a proper reprefentative for an honeft and free people.

I know, my friends, how you are likely to be befet with candidates. All that have any thing to afk, or any thing to fear, will now induftrioufly fue for, or at any rate purchafe, feats in parlement. Such men never confider whether they are qualified for the feats or not. It is fufficient, that they find the feats convenient and necefſary for their private purpofes. One looks for preferment, a penfion or a place; another flies from bailiffs into parlement. The a-gents of fuch men are already at work, and large fums are offered, upon a prefumption, that the next will be at leſt as long-lived a parlement, as the laſt. Thofe are dangerous men to fend into parlement: they can an-fwer no one end of the inftitution; they can

repre-.

reprefent onely their fordid felves. Sure you have had too many of this caft, ever to think of fending more of them out of the reach of juftice ! Thofe, who feek a feat as the means of preferment, are as dangerous as thofe who hope to hold their poffeffed places by parlementary corruption or fervility. You can never think of fuch men, but with contempt and deteftation. Your candidates muft be utterly unworthy, if they be not found difinterefted, honeft and free.

But, the more effectually to difappoint your purchafers upon a good life, let me recommend it to all the electors, who have retained their freedom and integrity, to revive the teft, I formerly propofed to be put to every candidate. The chief of thefe is a folemn promife to endeavor to bring parlements nearer the primitive inftitution, by making them, inftead of perrennial, contrary to law and reafon, triennial, or quadrennial at the moft, by a new law. Till this is done, the fpirit of the conftitution can never be reftored, nor your rights or liberties effectually fecured. This fhould be the great foundation of the work of reformation. But it is the ftone, which the modern political builders choofe to reject.

And

And now, my worthy countrymen, give me leave to addrefs myfelf in a more efpecial manner to my moft honored and beloved fellow-citizens of Dublin: a fenfe of the many patriot virtues that animated your generous breafts, and of the obligations and honors you heaped upon me, while lawlefs power was pleafed to permit me to breathe free air among you, is too deeply imprinted on mine heart, to be in any degree effaced by abfence, by diftance or by time. I muft ever, with refpect and gratitude, remember, that you called me from obfcurity, placed me in the confpicuous and honorable light of a candidate for one of the vacant feats of the capital city in parlement; that you diftinguifhed me with every mark of your approbation and affection, with public affurances of being elected; and you fupported your candidate, while your impious rulers retained any regard to fhame, to truth, to reafon, juftice or the laws. Before I can lofe fight of thofe marks of the public favor, or become infenfible of the matchlefs patriot fpirit that appeared predominant iu all claffes of the citizens of Dublin; let my right hand forget it's function, and my tongue cleave to the roof of my mouth!

That I have not forgot you, will appear by the various ftruggles I have made, firft to procure balm for the wounds given my country and you, through my fides. Application was made to every minifter here. None could be found, who could grant any terms, that an honeft and free man could accept. What man, confcious of his own innocence, and actuated by the left fenfe of virtue, could for any ends in life, ftoop to afk the tranfgreffing tyrants pardon? forfwear and facrifice the truths he had delivered, though of the utmoft importance to the king and people? and give the minifters affurance, that no fuch difagreeable, and to them, dangerous truths, fhould ever be told again? yet thefe were the beft terms I could obtain from a Britifh miniftry! and to thefe, I fhould then, or at any time, prefer an honeft exile, or any honorable death.

After thefe applications proved fruitlefs, and that I judged it difhonorable to purfue them further, I endeavored to give the alarm in London, and expofed the iniquitous and tyrannical meafures that ruined Ireland and her capital, and banifhed me; in hopes, they would take fome ftep to guard this kingdom and their city from the peftilence of corruption and flavery, raging in fo near a neighbouring country. You will hardly believe, that upon feveral trials, I could find no magiftrate nor recorder, that would prefent the dedication of a new edi-

I   tion

tion of my political papers to the corporation of the city, to whom I addreſſed it !

Of this, I afterwards complained, in an *Appeal to the Commons and Citizens*, in which I expoſed the negligence of ſome of their chief magiſtrates and their recorder, with ſome new injuries offered to the people of Ireland, conſequent to thoſe ſet forth, but diſregarded, in my dedication. But this produced no better effect.

Diſcouraged from hopes of obtaining my liberty upon honorable terms, I reſolved to go abroad to gain ſome improvements in my profeſſion. But, apprehenſive that my character would be further maligned by mine enemies, who were ready, upon the report, to inſinuate, that I fled from juſtice, and was now going to inliſt among the declared enemies abroad, I thought it right to lay the ſtate of my caſe before one of his Majeſty's principal ſecretaries of ſtate, and choſe to apply to the deſcendent of the great lord Ruſſel, conceiving ſome hopes of ſome redreſs, from ſo illuſtrious and powerful a perſon. The onely favor I ſtooped to aſk was *ſummum jus*, though generally allowed to be *ſumma injuria* ; a fair, but ſtrict trial, before competent judges and legal juries.----But this, it ſeems, was judged too great a favor for me. So I left this teſtimony of
my

my loyalty and innocence in the great officer's hands, and took my leave to go and finish my studies in foregne parts.

Since my return to this kingdom, I could, upon the strictest inquiry, find no honorable means of returning in safety to my country. Wherefore, taking the asylum which the laws give to all honest and loyal men here; I have since applied to the practice of my profession, and thank God! with some share of success and reputation. To this alone, was all my time and attention devoted, till my glad heart saw an opportunity offered, by heaven and the king, of offering some services to my poor country, and ruined city. And thus far, animated by his majesty's declaration, and hurried by a zeal to be of some public use, I had carried this address, to this length, before I could possibly have learned, that you, through so many passed years; and beset with such various scenes of oppression and perplexity, as you were, had been mindful of your old faithful servant, and again declared me a candidate for one of your vacant seats at the next ensuing general election.

From the generous regards and attentions you were pleased to pay me before, and the assurances my conscience gives me, that I could have done nothing to forfeit your favor; I must own, I expected, that you would

I 2   thus

thus demand the services, which I confefs I owe you, and thereby fhew fuch a fenfe of your own freedom and rights, and fuch a juft refentment of the violences offered you, when you were prevented electing me, or, I may fay, any other member; as would confound our enemies, and inable you to heal the wounds given the whole kingdom, as well as you, through my inconfiderable fides. Thefe, it is to be hoped, you will happily effect, by reinftating your banifhed fellow-citizen and candidate.

In all that I have hitherto been able to do for you, I lay no clame to any merit, nor demand any return. Had I been able to complete my beft intentions for you, I fhould have found all the reward I fhould ever feek or accept, within mine own bofom. The utmoft I did, or could hope to do, was but my duty, and that I could not decline, were there none other incentive, but the dictates of mine own confcience.

And as in your preferving your generous regards for a man oppreffed, ruined, and banifhed by lawlefs power, for his good intentions towards his country, and in this, as well as other inftances, purpofe to act upon unalterable virtuous principles; I cannot help looking upon your electing me your reprefentative in parlement, as the higheft honor I can receive, and muft confider the con-
fidence

fidence you mean to repofe in me, as the moft valuable and important truft that can be depofited in mine or any man's hands.

Therefore, though the talk of your re-prefentative be more than doubled, by my banifhment, and fince my exile ; duty and inclination, and ardent defire to ferve a brave, virtuous people, that dare be free, confpire to engage me to undertake the weighty charge, upon the fame principles, and from the fame motives, which I formerly layed down, in my perfonal and written addreffes, and in my letters to you, my moft honored fellow-citizens and friends.

My being thought of as a candidate, upon this occafion, muft perfuade me, that the fame virtuous principles and motives rule all your political conduct, as when a confide-rable majority in the greateft number of the moft populous corporations, declared pub-licly, voluntarily, for me. I fhould be dead to every fenfe of that public fpirit, that love of my country, which formerly ob-tained me the invaluable regards of the moft loyal and worthy citizens, could I be deaf to your calls, or did I not even anticipate your application to me, in any inftance, where I might judge it in my power to ferve you. Therefore, my beloved brethren and fellow-citizens, I thus rife and fet out to meet you. And, though the wicked projects of
our

our enemies have, by God's providence,
been fo far fruftrated, with refpect to me,
as to render an exchange of fituations, for
any thing to be expected in Dublin, in the
way of my profeflion, a very confiderable
facrifice of my private intereft; yet I fo far
hold it mine indifpenfable duty to anfwer
your patriot calls, feconding thofe of our
moft gracious Sovereign, that I do not he-
fitate one moment, in my determination,
but declare myfelf at once ready to imbarque
on a fea of troubles, to promote the common good ; and that at the peril of fuffering
fhipwreck, or living to want the neceffaries
of life : for, I am as fenfible as ever you
found me, perhaps more, that the firft duty,
a rational being owes, is to his God ; the
fecond is juftly challenged by his country.
When king and country, with infeparable
interefts, in one united caufe, call for the
fupport and affiftance of *every honeft man* ;
what *honeft man* can decline his utmoft fervices ? ———— I fhould hold myfelf utterly unworthy of being inrolled among the free
fubjects of fuch a king, or among my virtuous countrymen and fellow-citizens, did I
not look upon all that I now poffefs, or ever
hope to enjoy, even life itfelf, as a facrifice
to be duly, readily made, whenfoever it is
found neceffary for the good of my country.
    In this diffufive fenfe, you will fay, all
                                                    the

the kingdom has a right to demand my fervice. Undoubtedly. Therefore, if any of the many venal, and almoft depopulated boroughs fhould, at the godlike call of the king, receive a generous fpark, and kindle virtue enough to inable the majority to emerge from their corruption and flavery, fo far as to dare to choofe an honeft man ; if upon thefe principles, their election fhould alight upon me ; I fhould certainly hold myfelf bound to yield them due attention, and the beft fervices in my power. But, at the fame time, you muft know, that of all parts of the kingdom, Dublin muft have the firft clame to the utmoft fervices I may ever be able to offer. You likewife know, that the reprefentative of any part, even the moft mean, is a counfilor, a truftee and a guardian to the whole community.

You cannot, my worthy brethren, be yet fuppofed to have forgotten the doctrines I taught, and the principles upon which I proceded, and moved you, when you formerly did me the honor to fet me up a candidate. To fay, that thefe once obtained your approbation, would be too faint an expreffion. I may, of a truth, fay, you adopted them, and many of you were, in different manners and degrees, fellow-fufferers with me, for daring to differ from the eftablifhed modes and cuftoms of city and ftate *managers* or *under-*

undertakers, in profesling and aiming at freedom and truth.

It would be needlefs then to trouble you at this time, and in this manner, with repetitions of my fentiments upon this occafion. I hope thefe ftand recorded in your hearts, in indelible characters. But, if any be fo weak as to have forgotten them, they may be eafily recollected from my political papers, which I hope, I need not recite. If thefe and my general character do not give every elector as good affurance of my qualification, and as good fecurity for my conduct, as any other candidate has given, to fay no better; I fhall ever hereafter be filent on this head.

When attending the duties of your reprefentative would have been the left lofs and inconvenience to me, I held it inconfiftent with the principles I then did, and ever fhall, profefs, and which you generoufly countenanced and approved, to run into any degree of the deteftable methods of applying and foliciting for votes and interefts. I ever muft, and ever have thought it unjuft to lay any elector under any kind of reftraint in his choice. You may well remember, I onely folicited you to be wife and free in your choice; and, inftead of extorting, or even accepting promifes from any of you, I relinquifhed and gave up many

verbal

verbal and written promifes made me by feveral well-meaning, but miftaken electors. You then faw and approved my motives. They are ftill uppermoft in my bofom. But, were it poffible, that I fhould fwerve from thefe principles, the invariable purpofes of an honeft heart, it is not to be imagined, that, fituated as I am at prefent, at fo great a diftance from you, I fhould make any perfonal application for the favors of individuals.

It muft therefore fuffice, that I thus publicly declare, that I fhall hold myfelf in readinefs, at the fhorteft warning to engage in the fervice of my country, whenfoever and wherefoever I fhall be freely and legally called upon. I know nothing more that you have a right to demand or expect. You are to choofe reprefentatives for your city. If you do not choofe among the beft qualified and the moft likely to ferve you ; no degree of fenfe or honefty, of freedom or loyalty can be fuppofed to have fallen to your fhare. If electing me, be likely to prove conducive to your honor and the common good ; you muft choofe me. But if you cannot think thus of me, you are fools or flaves if you think of appointing me your delegate : For, I difdain to reprefent any but a fenfible, virtuous, loyal and free people, and fuch fhall ever command me.

K Hence

Hence you may judge, I mean to turn the tables, as you know I did before : I firmly purpofe, inftead of receiving, to confer the moft lafting obligations on my conftituents, if fuch I find ; by accepting, and with unalterable zeal and fidelity, difcharging the duties of a painful, laborious, and perilous office, which fools or knaves, flaves or parricides alone can make, or hope to find, in any fort lucrative. Such as thefe, may find it worth while, as well as neceffary, to beg and intreat, to imprefs or to purchafe votes ; they may be egregioufly obliged, while I choofe to be found among the number of the obliging. He, that thinks thus of himfelf, muft be better intituled to be folicited to ferve, than he that folicits to be elected. He may receive acknowledgments for his fervices from you ; but can offer none for your votes : For, he who looks for nothing more than being diftinguifhed from the multitude of electors, onely by *fuperior toils* and *an heavier weight of care*, cannot be fuppofed under the difagreeable neceffity of ftooping to folicite for the *painful preeminence.*

Therefore, let thofe who mean to inrich themfelves or their followers, at the expence of their country, by conniving at or joining in every infamous and deftructive fcheme, by avaricious or wicked minifters formed againft the rights and liberties of the people,

againft

againſt the honor and dignity of the ſovereign, and who are thus intereſted in coun-
teracting the glorious intentions of his Majeſty, or preventing his ever knowing a true
ſtate of the nation; let theſe fawn, cringe,
coax, cajole and corrupt; let them purchaſe,
by any ſordid means, the voices of the ignorant or unwary electors, that they may be
able to ſell their own, with the better grace,
though to the eſtabliſhing and confirming the
heavy and calamitous grievances, the abject
ſlavery and diſgrace, of the whole kingdom
and city, paſſed all proſpects or hopes of redemption. Such as can hearken to men of
this caſt, can hardly be worth any *honeſt
man*'s care; they muſt rather be the objects
of his moſt implacable deteſtation and contempt. If any ſuch be found in poor Dublin, God grant, the perfidious traitors may
never prove the majority! Thank heaven!
this is not to be feared : The far greater
number of the citizens are too ſenſibly touch-
ed with the violences offered them, with
their duties to their king and country, to
themſelves and poſterity, to need being urged
to act like ſenſible, honeſt and free men.
Were they otherwiſe, their election, inſtead
of an honor, would prove an indelible diſgrace to any ſenſible, honeſt man. Fools
and knaves can onely be repreſented by their
kind, properly. The honeſt muſt have honeſt
repreſentatives. May Dublin chooſe ſuch, or
one at all!　　　K 2　　　　To

To obey the dictates of an honeſt heart, zealous to ſerve you, and to anſwer the calls of my king and country, I judged it incumbent on me, knowing the various temptations and ſtratagems with which you will be aſſailed, to move you to exert your ſenſe of freedom and integrity, to a quickneſs and ſteadineſs, in the diſcharge of your laſt great duties to our commonwealth. You are now called on loudly, upon all ſides. You are offered the means of ſhaking off your ſhackles, of healing your wounds, bruiſes and putrifying ſores, and of bringing the cruel authors of your complicated diſtreſſes to confuſion and diſgrace. You cannot yet forget the fatal wouud given you, through my ſides. This is the onely time, in which you can hope to obtain a remedy. Now is the time to compel ſome regard to be payed to the redreſs of wrongs, to the reſtoring uſurped or betrayed rights and liberties.

In ſhort, my moſt dear countrymen and fellow-citizens, you are now offered the long with-held means of regaining and re-eſtabliſhing your rights and privileges, wreſted from you by lawleſs power; means of forming a new conſtitutional parlement; means of reſtraining your parlements within due bounds; means of reinſtituting the broken conſtitutions of the whole kingdom and city. You are invited to accept of the means
of

of obviating such impositions and misrepre-
sentations, as may be further attempted by
any future designing miniftry, as well as of
bringing former offenders to some degree of
the punifhment due to their moft atrocious
crimes. You are courted and prefled to take
into your own hands the means to vindicate
the honor of your late deceafed king, and to
fecure immortal renown to your prefent fovereign, who afks for, who *relies* upon the *fupport
and affiftance* of every *honeft man*, to enable
his majefty to perform and fulfil the great
bufinefs and purpofe *of his* royal *life, which
are to promote the happinefs and glory of his
people, univerfally*, by *preferving and ftrengthening the political conftitutions of his kingdoms*,
without diftinction. Who dare refufe to co-
operate with his patriot king?

You now have moral affurance, that nothing capable of effecting thefe great and neceffary purpofes can be wanting on the part
of the crown. You have the royal word,
that *preferving* and *ftrengthening the conftitutions, to the happinefs and glory of the fubjects*, are the moft firm purpofes of his majefty's heart, *the bufinefs of his life*. It is not
to be doubted, that thefe were the intentions
of the late king. Were they anfwered?
You know, that in fpight to the good intentions of the late kings, and quite unknown
to their majefties, the fad reverfe of thefe

pur-

purpofes was produced, the breaches of the conftitutions, and the wretchednefs and infamy, under which all fenfible men now groan. Are not then the great good intentions of the prefent patriot king as likely to be fruftrated, if you do not univerfally afford him the neceffary *fupport and affiftance* of *honeft men?* Prove yourfelves fuch then, my brethren, and fend to treat with and counfil the king, reprefentatives worthy of an *honeft* and *free* people, or look for endlefs deftruction and mifery, for you and yours.

I gratefully confefs, that I think your naming me in the number of the honeft and free men, on whom the king, as well as you, may rely, is doing me the greateft honor, whether the election fucceeds or not. But, judge what happinefs would attend your election of me, if I might hope to be one of the happy inftruments of redeeming my country and city, of *preferving and improving the* civil conftitutions? There can certainly be nothing wanting to produce thefe moft defirable great effects, than your electing men fit and qualified to be trufted. If Ireland and her capital have but the fenfe and virtue to choofe a worthy, a legitimate reprefentative; they can demand nothing neceffary for thefe great purpofes; that the king will not on his part, readily, gladly grant. Thus, by the proper exertion of an
ho-

honeft, patriot fpirit in your elections, you
fecure to yourfelves and pofterity, the king's
favor and protection, and regain and fecure
the happinefs, the glory, the liberties of
your kingdom and city. But, if you neglect
this, flavery, beggary, contempt and infamy,
muft moft defervedly be the portion of your
kingdom and city, to generations yet unborn. It is yours, now or never, to avert
the fatal doom.

As the qualifications and characters of
candidates are juftly fubjected to ftrict ex-
amination, to anfwer the purpofes of the
candid garb ; I freely fubject mine to every
fair teft. Do me but the juftice that criminals have a right to demand, though it has
hitherto been denied me ; let me have a
legal trial ; let me be heared, and let me
have fair open pleading, for and againft me,
before competent judges, and indifferent
jurors. Let my crimes be proved by faith-
worthy witneffes ; and let not the evidence
of witneffes, or the verdicts of jurors, or the
fentences of judges, which appear to be interefted in my condemnation, be recorded againft
me ! You cannot deny this piece of common
juftice to your enemies, to the worft of criminals. Remember how many among you
are fhamefully interefted in preventing my
return, much more my election into parlement. Thofe that injure, never forgive the
injured. He that ftabs innocence for the

guilty bribe, will furely dread feeing the murdered corfe, even at the general refurrexion. We have all been thus murdered, and are all long politically dead. Our gracious king, like a true vice-gerent of heaven, founds the inlivening trump, and calls us to a political refurrexion. Arife, anfwer, live and be free, be happy and glorious !

I have fpun out this Addrefs, from the overflowings of a zealous heart, and infenfibly protracted it, beyond the intended bounds. And yet, I have not time to abridge, or even to give it the correction which muft be neceffary for fo premature fo precipitate a performance. If it prove intelligible, I muft be content for the prefent. If it ferves to re-animate the long depreffed, though not extinguifhed virtues, that filled your generous breafts, when I faw you free ; if it roufes the thoughtlefs or unwary, to a fenfe and proper difcharge of their indifpenfable duties ; mine ends will be well anfwered ; and you will glorify God, blefs the king, be honeft, loyal and free ; and then, upon all occafions, you may reft affured of the utmoft fervices, as well as of the invariable affection, fidelity and zeal of,

My moft worthy countrymen,

Fellow-citizens and friends,

London,
Nov. 1, 1760.

Your moft devoted fervant,

C. LUCAS.

www.ingramcontent.com/pod-product-compliance
Lightning Source LLC
Chambersburg PA
CBHW020236090426
42735CB00010B/1722